Dan Richter

Fourteen Pearls of Wisdom for Improvisational Actors

This book is protected by copyright.
All rights to this work – including those regarding the translation, reprinting, reproduction, design, contents or parts thereof – are reserved. This work may not be reproduced or electronically edited, duplicated, or distributed in whole or in part without prior written permission.

© Dan Richter
Homepage: www.danrichter.de

Translation: Samantha Riffle

These fourteen pearls of wisdom are intended to provide stimulation and inspiration, to help break down mental blocks, and to make it easier to return to the fundamental virtues of improvisation.

Don't Be Afraid 5
Accept 8
Play the Game 11
Pretend 13
Apply Yourself 15
Listen 17
Notice New Forms 19
Support Your Partner 20
Support the Scene 21
Observe Your Environment 23
Study the Arts 24
Know the Ropes 26
Train Your Skills 28
Put on the Show That You Would Want to See 30

DON'T BE AFRAID

What are people most afraid of? Answer: the unknown.

And what are we dealing with when we improvise? Exactly: the unknown.

Overcoming our fear, turning it into something positive, leaving it behind us, and focusing on improvising – these are the challenges that we face again and again. We have to leap head-first into the scene with a resounding inner cry of "Woo-hoo!"

Our fear of the unknown often disappears if we simply act as though we're not afraid. It may be an old trick, but it's tried and true: As everyone knows, whistling past the graveyard will drive the evil spirits away.

A deep-seated reflex makes us skeptical, makes us say no and retreat when we encounter the unknown. Say yes. Move forward. Run the risk of happily crashing and burning.

But remember, beginners aren't the only ones who have to deal with fear.

Fear of Others Judging You

At some point in our lives, we all worry about looking awkward in front others. Even professional improvisers occasionally fall into the trap of playing it safe when some big shot is sitting in the audience whose opinion they value or fear. But a game dictated by fear will come across as deliberate and dull. You've got to shake your fears – and your own high expectations at the same time. Only play that is freed from its constraints will charm your audiences.

Fear of Your Own Judgment

Rationality can't justify playing, so the question often arises if what we're doing is actually any good. Of course, striving for high levels of artistic quality is always important, but we shouldn't allow it to get in the way of our playful instinct. That's why from time to time, you should take the opportunity to test boundaries, even if it means running the risk of failing; usually, you will achieve new levels of quality and develop new forms in the process.

Fear of the Greats

There are giants in every type of art. The question is whether you allow them to inspire you or intimidate you. Don't compare yourself to others too often. After all, vanity is another form of fear. Find your own voice, and trust it.

You should also check from time to time to see if fear has crept in through the back door. Fear can make headways in different forms, depending on what type of people we are. It manifests itself:

- when we frequently say "no",
- when we perform aggressively,
- when we perform cautiously,
- when we hold back too much and don't commit,
- when we try to maintain control,
- when we plan ahead,
- and when we seek a level of safety that simply cannot exist in improvisation.

Be brave, and everything will be OK.

ACCEPT

Just say yes. Acceptance is the foundation of all improvisation. In our everyday lives, we tend to be critical, assessing and weighing every decision we make. If we did so while improvising, it would prevent us from reaching the state of mental flow we need to perform. Instead, we have to happily accept the unknown and play with it. Open yourself physically and say yes. A *yes* opens doors, while a *no* closes them. Exercise your yes-muscle.

Accept Your Fellow Players' Offers

Regardless of how unimaginative or strange an offer may seem – accept it. Every time you accept, you are declaring your love to your fellow players. Every time you block their offers, you are slapping them in the face. The more often we practice saying yes and accepting, the easier it will become for us to develop a positive, creative relationship with our fellow players' offers.

Accept the Reality of the Scene Once It Is Established

When improvisers start to discuss the location, people, and situations in a scene, they never get around to the actual scene itself. So if you step onstage thinking you're the pizza delivery guy, but your fellow players decide you're the pope, then you're the pope.

Accept the Emotional Meaning

If your fellow player is playing a doctor and says: "I'm afraid it was too late for your son; we couldn't save him," you must allow yourself to be emotionally affected, rather than immediately blurting out, "Nooo! Why, God, why?!" Only when we are able to take emotional meaning seriously do our scenes have the chance to achieve depth.

Accept the Situation

Naturally, you should prepare your show well, examine the stage, sound, lights, and auditorium in advance, etc. But once the show begins, you have to accept the situation, even if it isn't ideal. If less audience members than usual show up, or if they don't seem to be in the best mood: accept it. If the microphone sound isn't perfectly balanced or the stage lighting doesn't show off your dazzling features quite the way you'd like: accept it. The situation is what it is. Play with it.

Accept Your Fellow Players

Sooner or later, every improv troupe will have to discuss issues such as its artistic path, rehearsals, money, or other minor details like stage outfits, emcees, or how to deal with the heckler who shows up in the front row of every performance. Discuss, find solutions, but also accept your fellow players' shortcomings – their vanities, idiosyncrasies, and weaknesses.

Acceptance Cannot Be Demanded

Be down-to-earth. Accept that your fellow players might occasionally block you onstage. You know yourself that even experienced professionals make that mistake sometimes. Make the best of it and play!

Accept Your Own Offers

Listen to yourself and be as receptive to your own offers as you would be to your fellow players'.

PLAY THE GAME

No matter what kind of game it is: get involved. Dive into it head first. Don't try to outfox the game, and don't put yourself above it. Don't try to turn it into something ironic. Fully commit yourself to it.

This applies to the "improv game" in the narrowest sense of the word as well as to improvised scenes and improvisation as a whole.

Find the game in open scenes.

Play with timing and rhythm.

Play with body and space, voice and sound.

Play with meanings.

Play with language.

Stay focused, but maintain a playful attitude toward everything you do onstage. Don't try to do something the "right" way, to accomplish something, or to check something off a list. Play with your "mistakes." Usually, audiences don't recognize a mistake until we indicate that it is one, such as by interrupting the game, laughing about the mistake, trying to correct it, etc.

A thousand things can hamper you: technical problems, financial pressure, too few audience members, your fellow players' egos, your own shortcomings. Don't let the difficulties stop you. Stay positive and play with them.

Accept the game. Play the game.

PRETEND

The stage belongs to you. Use it. Dive into the unknown. It's OK to fail when you take a risk, but if you mentally give up before you even start, you're only cheating yourself.

In improv – and particularly during live improv performances – we are confronted with unknown situations and have to be able to deal with them immediately, without forethought. We might have to play a seasoned airline pilot, improvise a poem, perform a piece in the style of Bertolt Brecht, or dance a pas de deux, for example.

Be brave and pretend!

If you think you can't do something, you can at least pretend to be able to do it. The actual ability to do it generally follows in the second step.[1] By pretending to be able to do something, we're not tricking the audience; rather, we're primarily tricking our own fear of failing. The audience is willing to accept a surprising

---

[1] Fake it 'til you make it.

number of things that happen on stage, as long as they're presented with confidence and panache. On the other hand, apologizing to the audience – by shrugging, raising our eyebrows, or even only feeling sorry inside – makes us look pathetic. Often enough, doing so is what actually *makes* audience members modify their opinions on what they've seen.

In fact, we make things easy for ourselves when we set the bar high! If I tell myself that I'm able to sing an opera aria, I *might* fail, but if I do, at least I'll do it with class and passion. However, if I throw in the towel right from the start, then I'm left with nothing but a pale imitation or a parody that falls flat. Improvisers will be disappointed, and audience members will be left with a bad taste in their mouths or, at best, will get a cheap laugh.

COMMIT

Treat every performance as though it could be the best one of your life. Avoid falling into the trap of simply slogging your way through a scene. If we only give fifty percent because the audience turnout isn't what we'd like it to be, or because it's "just a gig," we gradually destroy our love of improvising. In improv – and in art as a whole – you can't do things by halves. Throw yourself into every performance.

Use Your Physical Abilities

Theater is a physical art, so use everything at your disposal – your body, your voice, your endurance, and your strength – to give it your all.

Use Your Intellectual Capabilities

Each of us has above-average knowledge in at least one area. Don't discount these skills; use them in the game. Avoid playing the dunce – it won't make the scene funnier or more interesting. Use your brain.

Add Something

The principle on which every improv scene is based is known as "YES AND." If "YES" means acceptance, then "AND" represents the addition of a new offer for your partner. Stick with it. The more frequently you exercise your "and"-muscle, the better, faster, clearer, and more interesting the content you add will become.

Make Courageous Decisions

Nothing is duller than improvisers who can't make up their minds and end up carefully stewing in their own juices. As important as it is to cooperate with your partner, you shouldn't be *too* polite. A good improviser will find irritating offers more inspiring than pathetically treading water. Baby steps are OK, but why not take a leap once in a while, too?

LISTEN

Listen to your fellow players' offers. Stick with their ideas emotionally and mentally rather than trying to think something up yourself. You can get all the inspiration you need from them. Pay attention to content, but also to meaning.

The material that your partners set up is what you will have the chance to play with.

Allow yourself to be affected by what they say. Pick up on it immediately. Or later.

Reincorporate material. Recognizing and creating patterns isn't just a tool in comedy, storytelling, and improv; it is also an important aesthetic factor in art as a whole.

Practice listening. Practice remembering.

Don't think ahead; stay in the moment. If we listen carefully while simultaneously remembering what we've created, we are like someone who's paying attention while walking backwards: one eye firmly on the past, but still attentive to what's going on in the moment.[2]

Listen to the content. Refer to it.

Listen to the meaning. Does a sentence contain more than just what was said? Could it also have symbolic or metaphorical meaning?

Listen to style and form. Which poetic style are we dealing with? Which level of language? Is the scene treated more like cinematic realism, or is it more theatrical, with dialogue in verse?

Listen to the "music" of the scene. What sort of rhythm does the individual scene have? How is the language timed? If you consider all the scenes as a whole, what sort of rhythm do they have? Are loud or quiet tones dominant? As a player, I ask myself: Do I want to copy this, or contrast it? And of course: Listen to the musician's music.

Listening is also a decisive factor behind the story: If you listen well, then ideally, you should have everything that's happened and everything that's been said right in front of you. You can reincorporate certain elements to build a narrative bridge.

---

[2] I owe this metaphor to Randy Dixon.

NOTICE FORMS

Listening well gives us the chance to identify, create, and shape forms.

The start of every scene harbors the opportunity for us to compose countless new forms.

Listen to the content, and be prepared to reincorporate the material in a modified way. That's the first step toward making a comedy side-splittingly funny, or a tragedy harrowingly sad.

Find the game within the scene.

Find the game within the show.

Find the game within the game.

When a player repeats an element of a scene, it's a repetition. When it's repeated again, it becomes a game.

Be prepared to create new forms. Look out for forms that arise from playing with timing and space, with language and physicality.

The focus isn't just on what we present; how we present it – in what form – is equally important.

Strive for elegance.

SUPPORT YOUR PARTNER

You are improvising as a team, and you won't really shine unless you act like one. Support your partner and make him or her look good. Let go of your ego and its desire to impress the audience. Focus on performing together.

The best way to support your partner is to radically accept his or her offers, emotionally intensify them, and add something to them.

However, supporting your partner doesn't necessarily mean helping the character; rather, it means strengthening the character and the scene.

Play clear characters, and make clear offers.

Love your partner, and trust him or her.

If you are presented with a blind offer, accept it and make it more specific.

If you are presented with a strong offer, use its momentum.

Expect nothing. Give everything.

SUPPORT THE SCENE

What is the focus of the scene? Strengthen it. Ask yourself: What does the scene need?

Don't enter the stage without some sort of motivation; contribute something that the piece or the scene was missing up to now.

Thinking in terms of contrasts can often help.

Energy: If the characters have lacked energy up to this point, then the scene could probably use some momentum now.

Emotion: If the scene has been gloomy up to this point, then you probably need to play a positive character.

Meaning: If the scene is treading water, then your fellow players need you to demonstrate the consequences.

Characters: Is the scene missing the character it needs to round off the story? Jump in. But keep in mind: Not every character mentioned in the scene needs to actually show up. Be brave enough to allow those gaps. In large ensembles, on the other hand, it can often be smart to piggyback on the momentum of the group's size and to simply copy what others are doing. The same rule applies to the beginning of a scene: If your partner mimes peeling potatoes, simply copy him or her. You'll figure out what to add by listening and making use of the scene's energy.

OBSERVE YOUR ENVIRONMENT

Don't be afraid of clichés, but don't feel the need to chase after them, either. Clichés are the enemies of truth. Draw on reality:

How do people behave?

How do they talk?

What are their weaknesses, and what makes someone a hero?

Reality should be the primary influence on your performance. Beware of the imitations presented by the media; sooner or later, they will invariably lead to clichés. Even imitating other improvisers will usually restrict your own abilities. Pay more attention to the annoying bus driver than to the TV star.

Where can we find everyday stories? From fun little anecdotes to difficult moral decisions, our day-to-day lives provide us with the realistic foundation that our stories and characters need in order to become more than just hot air.

Stay informed. Take an interest in politics and science.

STUDY THE ARTS

Keep an eye on the arts and be open to new art forms.

Study Literature

How can I use narrative and poetic tools for our purposes? What linguistic forms and styles can I adopt? Re-read poems. Read comics, read philosophy. Read scripts and plays.

Study Films

Today, our expectations regarding narratives are strongly shaped by film. Which narrative tools can I skillfully implement on the improv stage? Pay attention to elements such as editing and time skips. How do genres actually work (as more than just the clichés in our minds)?

Study Stagecraft Carefully

Learn from theater that isn't improvised. Which dramaturgical tools can we use? How does stage language work? Observe the lighting and sound effects. Observe abstract forms of performance, such as dance theater. Observe acting techniques. Pay particular attention to pantomime – how can we use it? Enjoy smaller-scale performing arts in moderation – comedy, juggling, magic. How do they interact with the audience?

Study Music

Pay attention to songs in particular. Listen to everything, from oratorios to free jazz to death metal. Try it out, parody it, imitate it, absorb it. Mimicry gives you access to styles that you might otherwise dismiss.

Study Unrelated Art Forms

Architecture, sculpting, and painting can influence you, even if you can't always find a direct use for them in improv. Keep an open mind.

And of Course, Watch as Much Improv as You Can

Don't be too disappointed about bad shows; you will probably learn just as much from them as you would from good ones. Ask yourself: Why does one thing work when another thing doesn't? Don't judge too quickly. Learn from the performers' attitudes toward improvisation, learn from artistic structures. Avoid the temptation to copy good performers, ensembles, shows, etc. down to the last detail. Otherwise, you will wind up doing nothing but imitating their mannerisms.

Try things out. Copy something and do it completely differently – in your own way. Explore your options, and give them your own voice.

KNOW THE ROPES

Unfortunately, the improv world is crawling with clumsy surgeons, ignorant bureaucrats, and scenes revolving around "my first day at the office".

Know your settings. Know where items are located. Don't waste your improv time looking for something when it could just as easily be lying right next to you.

Define what you don't know. When your partner makes a blind offer, define it quickly rather than asking.

Answer, don't ask. And if you have to ask, add something relevant.

Try not to play idiots or drunks too often. The dumber the character, the more superficial it is. When you play children, don't play them stupid – play them appropriately intelligent.

Incorporate your own knowledge. Don't be afraid of the gaps in your knowledge – we all have them. If you include knowledge from your day-to-day life, the scenes will become more malleable and believable.

Play specifically. The general is the enemy of art, the specific its friend.

Use your special knowledge. Everyone has areas where they know more than others. Don't be afraid to incorporate that expertise. You can do it in a completely unpretentious way: For example, if you're an expert in different species of birds, you can simply name them in passing.

Don't shy away from addressing or philosophizing on "big" issues onstage. You can't go wrong; after all, you're playing a role.

Don't play beneath your level. If you're a good singer, don't sing off-key on purpose just to flirt with dilettantism.

TRAIN YOUR SKILLS

Many improvisers believe that the only way to develop as a player is to keep learning new games and show formats. While doing so may be useful, the decisive factor in a performer's development is how often he or she exercises his or her acting, narration, and improvisational skills. This kind of training never ends. If we want to avoid becoming stiff and stocky, we need new sources of inspiration, as well as feedback from our colleagues and teachers.

As an Actor:

Train your voice.

Keep your body flexible.

Always be on the lookout for new characters. Find them in animals, items, and particularly in real people. "Real" means finding inspiration in people from your actual life, rather than in the cliché characters of the indirect world of film, comedy, television, and improv.

As an Improviser

Practice spontaneity. Every once in a while, replay some beginner games.

Exercise acceptance and commitment.

As a Narrator and Director

Practice storytelling. Every day. Even if you're talking on the phone about something that happened to you, make the story exciting.

Practice placing breaks in your story.

Practice different styles.

Build on your strengths, and work on your weaknesses.

PUT ON THE SHOW THAT YOU WOULD WANT TO SEE

Asking yourself, "What does the audience want?" will always lead to cheap artistic opportunism, the result of which is that you will cater to the lowest common denominator in the crowd. The game will become stale, predictable, and uninspired.

Conversely, if you only think from the stage downward, the improvisation will tend toward the incomprehensible and aloof.

Art is communication. Particularly when you put on shows regularly, you have a good chance of attracting the audience that you deserve.

So ask yourself: What kind of show would *you* want to see? What you make of it can be mass-market or avant garde. Either way, you and your audience will have a satisfyingly mutual artistic understanding.

Your own taste can be a good guide, as long as you remain open to new things.

Dan Richter, improviser and author, lives in Berlin, Germany.

Herstellung und Verlag:
BoD – Books on Demand, Norderstedt
ISBN 978-3-7322-7364-5